THE ART OF POSITIVITY

35+ HOPEFUL COLORING PROJECTS

Get Creative 6

NEW YORK

70118294

Introduction

I created the art for this book during the COVID-19 pandemic of 2020. While I was quarantined at home, I started to draw a daily page that featured a quote I found comforting. After a while, my friends and family who saw the pages clamored for their own pages to color. That's how this book was born.

Coloring is a wonderful way for people of any age to find comfort, relaxation, and creativity. You can choose the art supplies that suit your fancy. Who doesn't get a flashback to childhood when they open a new box of crayons, and get a whiff of their distinctive smell? Who doesn't get a thrill when they open a box of markers or colored pencils, and see that rainbow of colors?

There's no right or wrong way to color. You can choose whatever colors you like. I've varied the complexity of the drawings in this book. When you have a day where you feel stressed, and it's difficult to focus, choose one of the easier pictures. It's a meditative, calming activity.

I am so happy you've chosen this book to add to your collection! I hope you enjoy using it as much as I enjoyed creating it.

—Jane Maday

Tools and Materials

These are some of my favorites, but you might find others you prefer.

Colored pencils come in a huge variety of colors and types, from quite hard to very soft. My favorites are in the middle range. Soft pencils can be very good if you suffer from sore hands. If you like blending, choose a softer pencil. You can also use water-soluble colored pencils for more watercolor-like effects.

Watercolor markers with brush tips work like a paintbrush and rarely bleed through paper, unless it's quite thin. Water-based markers (different from watercolor markers) often have a bullet-shaped tip. Use these with caution, because in my experience, they tend to tear up the paper quite quickly.

Alcohol markers will bleed through almost any paper. However, they come in a wide variety of colors and blend very smoothly, so just be sure to put a protective sheet under any page you're coloring with them.

Gel pens are a type of paint pen. They're good for small areas, or for adding your own details. Gel pens and markers work well together, as you can use markers to color large areas, and use gel pens for the details.

Crayons are a good old favorite. Sometimes taking yourself back to childhood can be relaxing and comforting. Just for fun, I like to use water-soluble crayons sometimes.

Blending tools are good to have in your arsenal. For watercolor markers or water-soluble pencils, you want a medium-size round brush with a good point for small areas. Buy a proper artist's watercolor brush, as those made for kids don't hold much water or come to a good point. Blending pens are markers with a solvent inside instead of color. Choose one with a fairly soft tip. If the tip is too hard, there's a risk it will roughen up the paper surface. For both these tools, you don't need to apply much pressure. A delicate stroke is best.

Shading

Shading is a great way to add depth to your coloring. My favorite method is to color the base color with a marker, then shade with colored pencils. Choose your base color, then one or two darker colors for shading. You can also buy blending pens for either markers or colored pencils that help make a smooth blend.

Alcohol Markers with Colored Pencil Shading

1 Color the top of the mushroom with yellow, orange and red alcohol markers. They will bleed through paper, so put a sheet of scrap paper underneath if you use them.

2 Color the rest of the mushroom with markers. Blend the top with a colorless blender.

3 Choose darker tones and add shading with colored pencils using short circular strokes. Choose which side you want the light to come from (I chose the left side).

4 Blend with a colorless blender pen. Add highlights (if desired) with a white paint pen.

Watercolor Markers

1 Color the butterfly with various blues and grays.

2 Choose darker tones and add shading. Your strokes should be light and go outward from the center. If you release the pressure at the end of each stroke, the stroke will taper.

3 Blend with a colorless blender pen or damp brush. Don't have your brush too wet, or the paper will buckle. Use featherlight strokes, or you might end up picking up too much of the pigment. Add highlights with a white paint pen, if desired.

Water-Soluble Colored Pencils

 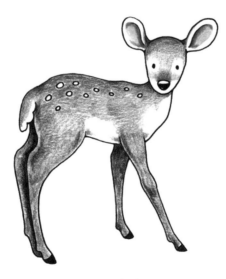 

1 Color the fawn with your base colors.

2 Choose the darker tones, and add shading. For a smooth effect, use soft circular strokes. Don't press too hard or you will burnish the paper.

3 Using a damp brush and featherlight strokes, blend the colors. Your brush should not be sopping wet, and your strokes should be light, or you will lift too much of the pigment.

Keep moving
FORWARD

Little by little
you can go far

Hang in there.

Nothing can bring you peace but yourself

Ralph Waldo Emerson

Dance in the puddles.

You can never make a CUP OF TEA large enough OR A BOOK long enough TO SUIT ME

C.S. Lewis

An Early Morning WALK

is a BLESSING FOR THE WHOLE DAY

-Thoreau

For I know
PLANS
to give you
HOPE
and a
FUTURE
Jeremiah 29:11

BEE HAPPY

A flower
BLOOMS
For its own JOY

-Oscar Wilde

ONCE
YOU CHOOSE
HOPE
anything
IS POSSIBLE.

Christopher Reeve

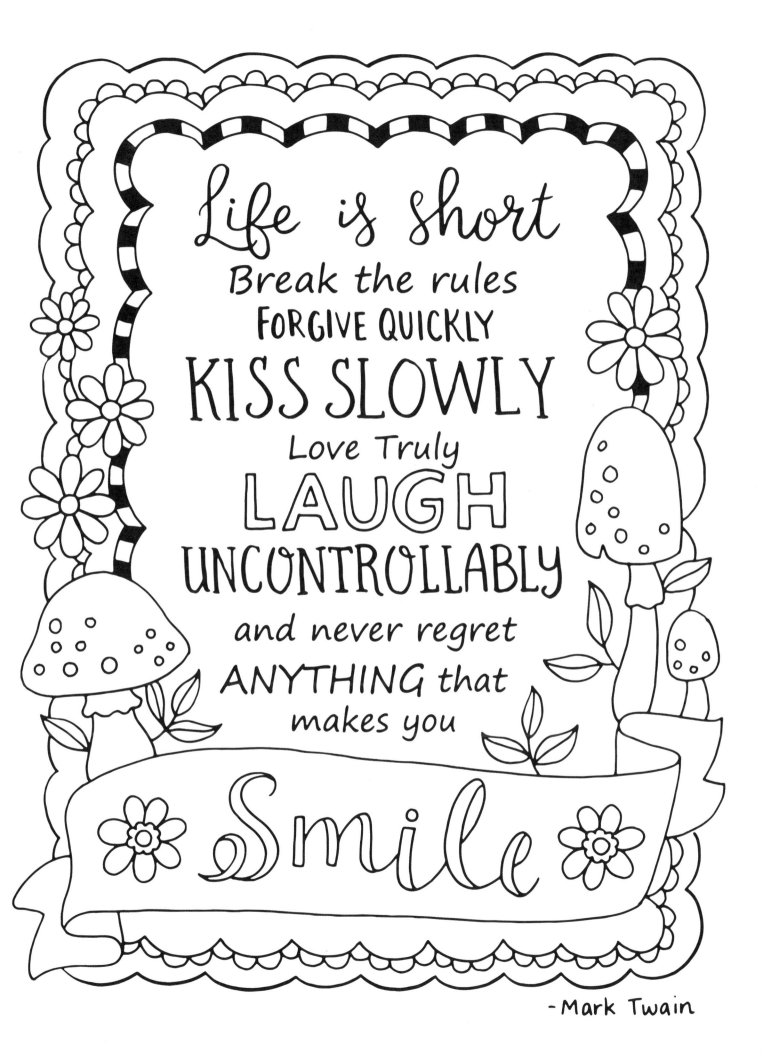

What seems to us AS BITTER TRIALS are often Blessings IN DISGUISE

Oscar Wilde

This book is for my sister, Anne,
for always being an inspiration.

About the Author

Jane began her career at fourteen years of age, as a scientific illustrator for the University of Florida. After receiving a bachelor's degree from the Ringling College of Art and Design, she was recruited by Hallmark Cards, Inc. as an illustrator. Jane left the corporate world after her children were born, and moved to beautiful Colorado. Her work has adorned dozens of books, collector plates, ornaments, cards, t-shirts, garden flags, jigsaw puzzles, and many more. In addition to the breathtaking Colorado landscape, she has two children, a menagerie of animals, a garden for inspiration, and a husband to share it all.

Thanks to Pam and the gang at SoHo Publishing, with much appreciation for all their support!

Get Creative 6
An imprint of Mixed Media Resources
104 W. 27th Street, 3rd Floor, New York, NY 10001
sixthandspringbooks.com

Editor: Pamela Wissman
Art Director: Irene Ledwith
Designer: Danita Albert
Chief Executive Offer: Caroline Kilmer
President: Art Joinnides
Chairman: Jay Stein

Copyright © 2021 by Jane Maday
All rights reserved. No part of this publication may be reproduced or used in any form or by any means—graphic, electronic, or mechanical, including photocopying, recording, or information storage-and-retrieval systems—without written permission of the publisher.

The designs in this book are intended for the personal, noncommercial use of the retail purchaser and are under federal copyright laws; they are not to be reproduced in any form for commercial use. Permission is granted to photocopy content for the personal use of the retail purchaser.

Manufactured in China

5 7 9 10 8 6

First Edition